EduCation

Train ! Play ! Love !

Complete training guide

for beginners

Full Color Photo illustrated book

Gary Rich

Table of Contents

DESCRIPTION

D o you own a cat that is full of fun and mischief? Would you like to train it to become receptive to basic commands?

This book holds all the answers!

For many years most people assumed that cats could not be trained, that they were too independent of humans and aloof to even consider becoming more than simple companions that accepted our hospitality and gave little in return. But those assumptions no longer apply.

Inside this book, How to Educate Your Cat: Teach, Play, Train and Solve Behavior Problems to Care For Standard and Hemingway Cats, you will discover a whole new side to our feline friends, while tips and ideas that cover:

- The different breeds of house cats
- Secrets and behavior characteristics of domestic cats
- Socializing with your cat
- Training techniques
- Equipment to aid training
- The amazing abilities of Hemingway cats
- Tricks and games for kittens
- Training for older cats
- And more...

For hundreds of years we resigned ourselves to the belief that cats could not be trained, but now Gary Rich is showing you not only how we can communicate with them, but also train and play with them, according to their traits and characteristics, producing some incredible results along the way.

With How to Train Your Cat you will learn which types of cats are easiest to train and allow you to enjoy a much richer and far more fun relationship with your pet, that you will both enjoy.

Scroll up and click Add to Cart for your copy now!

ABOUT THE AUTHOR

Gary Risman (Gary Rich) started his career working in the sales industry. At first, he endured many hardships; however, his hard work and dedication led him to become very successful.

He received numerous awards as a top sales associate, as well as a top manager. Besides, he was recognized as the best performer in these fields in his region and even nationwide.

Soon after that, Gary organized a large team that set prominent records in direct sales. In 1999, he received the highest award and title, "Golden Crown Prince," for the US and Canada's best performing location. He was featured on the cover of *Rexevents* magazine, a monthly publication by the "Ross" company. For 20 years, Gary learned from Zig Ziglar, billionaire Berel Walk, completed multiple training sessions, and was a top salesperson and distributor. Gary then opened a successful chain of locations on the East Coast.

As a result, Gary's life was filled with many events, but not all of them were pleasant. At the end of the 1990s, he lost everything, including his house. He lost his team and his office network, which he spent many years building. Gary was left without a home or car; his family fell apart, his health deteriorated, and he struggled just to find a reason to keep going. He was left with nothing; he was utterly alone, with no money or a way out. However, thanks to the knowledge from his mentors, he was able to bounce back resiliently and overcome the crisis in just 90 days.

He's presently one of the most popular international motivational speakers in the world. He has inspired thousands of listeners, who went on to build positive, successful lives, rooted in hard work, grit, mindfulness, and dedication.

FOREWORD

In this book, we will teach you how to effectively socialize with your felines, to become a happy and responsible pet parent. You will learn not only training techniques, but also the best tricks and entertaining games to use with your kittens. Cats are not like children, eventually tiring of dated games; they are always ready to play and will delight you with their mischief until old age.

One type of cat is typically more easily trained than any other: polydactylous, cats born with extra toes on one or more of their paws. Polydactyls can be born into any breed, so count your feline's toes, just in case. It could be that it is one of these smart, highly active cats.

As soon as newborn kittens open their eyes for the first time, they are ready to explore the world around them. They are unlikely to simply sit still in their boxes or carriers. If you have a few kittens in your home, your little gang will crawl into all the most secluded corners, climb your ceiling-high curtains, and jump onto your tallest cabinets or dressers with ease. You may stumble upon a sleeping kitten in your shoe, jacket pocket, coat, or even your purse. Kittens know how to entertain themselves, and at times it seems they don't need a master.

However, if you offer your kitten a small piece of paper to play with or ball to chase, they won't refuse and could be occupied for hours. A kitten that has lived with a person since birth should grow up to become a domesticated, well-adjusted cat. And if it likes a person, it may approach and rub against their leg, thereby letting its human know that they are also a member of the pack. On the other hand, if one does not properly socialize or play with their kittens, hold them, and learn the individual characteristics and peculiarities of their new family members, then they will certainly grow into an unsociable, unkind, almost wild animal.

Kittens, like small children, need to be offered a useful activity, some kind of game, to occupy their time. If left to their own devices, they will start to misbehave, tearing and chewing up the furniture. Some craftsmen build pet playgrounds for their cats, often including stairs and thick ropes hanging from the ceiling so the kittens can climb on them instead of the curtains. More ropes are wound around a wooden cylinder so the furry athletes have something to sharpen their claws. Observation platforms may be built up high near the ceiling, so the kittens are not tempted to jump on the cabinets.

WHY DO KITTENS AND CATS LOVE TO PLAY?

For felines, games are fun and beneficial at the same time. By playing, they constantly train their muscles and have fun, and happy cats make happy owners. Through a variety of games, kittens receive vital information about the world around them. In a playful way, they familiarize themselves with adult life, imitating the behavior of their mothers and honing their hunting skills. A tiny kitten is born.

Kittens are born blind, but with teeth and claws. After two weeks, they open their eyes for the first time and begin inspecting the world around them with surprise. Then they try to walk, hesitantly at first, swaying side to side. A month later, the healthy kittens are placed in the kind arms of their new owners who would like to know: Should one even be playing with their kittens at such a young age? And what kind of games are appropriate?

At just one month old, kittens are already jumping, climbing on upholstered furniture and curtains, and zooming around their homes with boundless energy. They begin to eat soft food. A kitten listens closely to every rustle. The hunter's instinct is triggered, and it can be used.

Put the kitten on the floor or carpet. Take a string and dangle it in front of the kitten's face, swinging it slowly from side to side, like a pendulum, allowing the kitten to focus on the string. Sooner or later the hunter's instinct will take over, and the kitten will try to grab the string with its claws.

Or try pulling the string in front of the kitten, which will surely be interested in the crawling snake and try to bite it, though you might have to try several times to get the little one to focus on the string.

If a kitten could talk, this would be its primary question. But, alas, it only meows, so you, as the owner, are left to come up with games yourself and find those most entertaining to your feline. Here are some ideas to get you started:

Golden ray of sunlight. For this game, you can use a laser pointer or a small flashlight. Aim the beam on the floor in front of the kitten and slowly guide it right, left, and around. Naturally, it will try to catch the beam. On a sunny day, try to use a small mirror or some other reflective surface to redirect a sunbeam in the direction of your kitten. Guide the rays around the kitten and it will gladly rush to catch them. Remember to never shine a light in your cat's face or eyes! Doing so can blind or cause irreparable damage to your furry loved-one.

The cardboard house. Everyone knows cats love boxes. They will hide in them, nibble at them, and put so many miles on the boxes that they may soon need replacing. Take an ordinary cardboard box and cut geometric shapes of varying sizes in the sides. Put a treat or favorite toy in the box and watch as the kitten tries to navigate its way in and out of the holes, or tries to pull the reward out with its claws.

A train of boxes can be created by simply cutting holes connecting the boxes and placing a treat or toy inside. Your cat will gladly explore the train, running and climbing from car to car.

Instead of boxes, you can also use a large paper bag. Throw toys or paper balls rolled to various sizes in the bag. Your kitten will be glad to play with them inside the bag. Do not use a plastic bag! Your cat can suffocate in the bag or start chewing it and accidentally swallow pieces of plastic.

Jumper. Take any small rubber or tennis ball and bounce it off the floor onto the wall. Your kitten will rush to the wall to try to catch the ball.

Shoelace. Tie a shoelace or long bit of string to your ankle and play with your kitten, slowly walking around your home. The string will follow you, and your kitten will likely fall in line behind it, trying to catch the string in its claws or teeth. Keep an eye on your feet! Do not step on your kitten in its excitement to catch the string.

A ball of yarn accidentally dropped on the floor can make a great toy for your pet. It will happily bat it across the floor, wrapping the legs of tables and chairs.

Worm under the rug. Stretch a length of string or wide ribbon under a rug so that it peeks out from both sides. Pull one end until the other disappears under the rug; then do the opposite. Repeat this and your kitten will rush from side to side trying to catch the string.

The Teaser is the simplest toy. Take a piece of paper or a bright candy wrapper and fold it like an accordion. Secure the accordion to a length of string or thread and then attach it to a doorknob or handle. Do not make a teaser out of feathers or very narrow ribbons. Your feline may accidentally swallow them in its excitement.

A TASTY PUZZLE

You can find some interesting toys in pet stores designed to challenge your pet to retrieve a treat somehow lodged inside the toy. Simply insert the treat, offer it to your kitten, and watch. For a while, enjoy the peace and quiet as your whiskered friend tries to solve the puzzle. If you are so inclined, you can try crafting one of these toys yourself.

MR. WHISKERS GOES HUNTING

The feline tribe's favorite activity is hunting, so make sure your canaries, parrots, and hamsters are secure in their cages. For this game you can buy a toy mouse from the store. Any kind of a childs wind-up toy should also work. Or you can sew a mouse from old fur mittens, gloves, or an old hat. Simply sew a string onto the end and drag it around your home. Home craftsmen may also make their own robotic "prey" for their kittens, if they are mechanically inclined, though be sure the toy does not contain any choking hazards for your little one.

CAT TENNIS

To play this game you will only need an ordinary tennis ball. Just throw it on the table or floor and it will catch the attention of your pet. You can also roll the ball across the floor and allow your cat to chase it and try to take it in its teeth.

GO FISH!

Take a long stick, telescopic fishing rod or pointer, and fasten your cat's favorite toy or tasty treat on the end. Sit back in your chair or on the couch and cast your line, lowering the bait to the cat's level. When it tries to grab it, raise the rod up sharply, and repeat.

FETCH!

Cats are not dogs, of course, but they can also fetch toys on command. By now you've seen how happy your kitten runs off after a ball or toy. You can buy a rubber ball or make your own out of crumpled up paper or a piece of foam. However, a paper ball should never be made from newspaper. Printing ink contains lead, and as your cat carries the ball around in its teeth, small amounts of the ink particles may enter its body. This could have negative consequences for the health of your feline.

Roll the ball across the floor, and your fur baby will quickly take interest. Allow your kitten to play with the ball to its heart's content, and when it has burned off sufficient energy, lie down next to your pet and send the ball forward again several more times. Obeying instinct, it will take the ball in its teeth, and, when it does, call your pet's name, and it will come to you and drop the ball next to you.

You can replace the ball in this game with round chips cut from cardboard. Just throw them to your kitten, and it will try to catch them. Some adult cats will even jump to catch the pieces in their paws. Your cat may then take the piece in its teeth and bring it to you. You will know if the cat likes this game, because, when they see you pick up the pieces next time, they will wait for you to begin throwing them. Clean up, however, will be left to you.

HIDE AND SEEK

Did you know it's possible to play hide and side with your kittens? When your pet sees you, hide behind a door or piece of furniture, wait a bit, and stick your head out and say, "Peek-a-Boo." Quickly hide again. Repeat several times, always looking your pet directly in the eye. Sooner or later it will be interested in what you're doing and approach. It may meow, or it may just look at you. Move around the room and quickly find another hiding spot. Repeat the process, again looking the kitten in the eye and saying, "Peek-a-Boo" or "Here I am!"

It can be hard to draw a clear line between cat games. Often one game may contain elements of another. Develop new games for your pet; be creative and experiment. The most important thing is to learn specifically what kind of games your kitten *wants* to play.

CAN I USE A LASER POINTER TO PLAY WITH MY CAT?

You may, provided you are careful. Be sure to never shine the light in your pet's eyes, or it may damage or even blind them. It is best to use green lasers with your cat as they can see them even during the day.

Close the windows beforehand, so the kitten doesn't fall out in its excitement. The laser is still an imperfect toy because it cannot be caught and held in the paws, and, as such, your cat will not find a satisfying "end" to the game. When it has played enough, shine the beam on a treat or favorite toy that your cat can "catch" and take in its teeth.

THERE'S A HUNTER GROWING UP IN YOUR HOME

By now your kitten has grown up almost unnoticed. Your furry little one is now already four to five months old. In nature, felines this age try to catch flies, wrestle with one another, and poke their noses in everything they can. But how can you develop your kitten's hunting instinct at home without risking harm to furniture, clothing, shoes, or other members of your family?

As an owner you will have to become a mother cat and play hunting games with your kitten. It needs to develop its abilities in hunting, stalking its prey, waiting in ambush, and chasing. It must learn to catch prey and attack. In natural conditions, a mother cat will catch a mouse and use it to teach her kitten.

But what are owners to do in domestic conditions? Go hunting for a mouse themselves? That isn't necessary. You may buy a wind-up toy mouse or use your imagination and ingenuity to craft one at home. You may use many improvised materials including yarn, paper, feathers, or bits of fabric. Just be certain that no choking hazards are present.

One piece of advice: let the kitten know who the boss of the house is. Always immediately put a stop to any display of hunting instinct towards your person. Never allow your kitten to bite or scratch you or any members of your family.

CHOOSING AN AGE-APPROPRIATE GAME FOR YOUR CAT

How you play with and train your feline will depend entirely on its age. At one month, kittens are still exploring the world around them without causing much harm to their surroundings. You need only play simple games with them. At five or six months, a kitten is a veritable troublemaker, and if you have several at home, they're closer to a gang. They need to be offered games that will hone their hunter's instincts, but not to the detriment of the furniture.

Adult cats also love to play, and they want to be winners. With enough imagination, an owner can come up with new games and entertainment, or just complicate some of the simpler games.

PRECAUTIONARY MEASURES

Before playing with a kitten, inspect the room. Move all unnecessary items, chairs, and tables from the play area, especially if the room is particularly small. Grown felines are agile and nimble. They have a natural survival instinct and will avoid all obstacles in their path.

Little kittens, on the other hand, are still clumsy. Remove all toys and small items from the floor if any are scattered about. You should also remove any sharp items that could potentially cut your kitten. And, as always when playing with a kitten, watch your step!

If at some point during the game your kitten suddenly grabs your hand with its claws, do not yell at or hit your pet. Simply freeze, and the kitten should retract its claws.

A CAT'S LIFE IS ONE BIG GAME

The feline is one of the most naturally curious animals. It explores its surroundings with the help of its extraordinary sense of smell. Getting to know new items can be like a game for your kitten. When you buy something from the store, offer it to your kitten to smell. If you are cooking, offer some to your furry taster to give a test smell. Encourage your feline's curiosity and remember the lesser known ending to the proverb *Curiosity killed the cat, but satisfaction brought it back.*

IF YOUR CAT WON'T PLAY

This is alarming behavior. It could be that your pet just isn't in the mood. Or it could be that something is bothering it, or it is in pain or sick. Contact a veterinarian as soon as possible. Stress can occur in cats just like in humans. Be more attentive, pet your furry friend more, and pamper it with treats.

If your pet won't play with a toy, it could be that they simply don't like that toy. It could be the smell, color, size, texture, or sound of the toy. Buy several different toys and offer them to your kitten one at a time. Do not throw all of them down at once or your cat will quickly lose interest in all of them.

With age, cats typically become less playful. Sometimes, however, old Simba will suddenly start running and frolicking with the kittens. Be happy – your cat is healthy. Take the initiative and try to play more often. Buy your adult cat a new toy or make one yourself.

"The cat to a certain extent retains its independence, in whatever circumstances it is, and obeys a person only insofar as it finds it beneficial for itself."

Brehm,
"Life of Animals"

Dogs, due to peculiarities of their nervous systems, are easier to train than other pets. But what about cats? Can they be trained? Yes, but the methods of training them differ greatly from those applied to the training of other animals.

We've seen cats stare at us, with unblinking round or slanted eyes, studying who is a friend and who is a foe. Why do cats immediately approach certain people while avoiding others, hissing at them and arching their backs with puffed up tails? If you want to know the kind of person standing in front of you, just ask your cat. It has the same inherent character traits as a person: jealousy, resentment, anger, joy, and love. But it lacks a sense of shame. Therefore, it is useless to shame your feline in front of an accident left on the floor by sticking its nose in the accident. Your cat will genuinely not understand what is wrong, be hurt, and abandon you. "I am a cat. I go where I please, and I walk alone." This is the credo of the feline tribe.

WHY YOU SHOULD TRAIN YOUR CAT

Training has two goals:

1. ***Socialization of the animal*** - training according to the specific rules you've set in your home. For example, your pet should respond to its name, know where to eat, rest, and use the bathroom, and use only the designated scratching post to sharpen its claws.
2. ***Learning simple tricks*** - beneficial for developing your pet's intelligence. This can bring variety to both the life of the cat, especially if it is an indoor cat, and to the owner.

Trained pets are sociable and cause less problems in daily life. They can be safely left at home. A trained cat is easy to transport in a car with or without a cat carrier. Trained cats also react more calmly to strangers precisely because they are closer to their owners. Trained cats can be taken to the veterinarian or on a trip with ease.

World-famous Russian trainer Yuri Kuklachev believes that a cat shouldn't even be praised in the presence of another cat. The cats may begin to tear one another apart because of feelings of jealousy. With cats, showing praise or extra attention to one will likely have the others seeking the same validation.

Kuklachev, by the way, does not train his pets, but merely observes their habits. His business card – a cat in a Russian sundress and handkerchief sitting on a pot – was inspired by a simple kitchen saucepan. Yuri came home one evening to find his cat, Strelka (Arrow), sitting in the pan.

Kuklachev turned the pan over and Strelka jumped out, but as soon as he returned the pot to the table, the cat jumped back in the pot. Several times Kuklachev overturned the pot, and every time Strelka returned to his new favorite spot in the house. This trick became the basis of Kuklachev's famous circus act.

Ultimately, training cats is most likely all a game to them. You can't yell at them, and certainly can't hit them. Your pet will run away and want little more to do with you. A cat is not a dog and does not take orders.

There are different principles of and approaches to training cats and dogs. Don't forget that cats are highly independent creatures. In contrast to dogs, they are more attached to their home than they are to their owner. A cat chooses its owner itself, as they say. They are slow to submit to training.

To teach them the simplest commands, an owner must stock up on perseverance, time, patience, love, and treats to encourage their cat. What tips should you follow when training your furry pet?

1. Remember that your cat is a living creature and not an object. Treat it as a partner, not as a subordinate to be ordered around. Watch your cat carefully and learn its likes and dislikes. I would even suggest that the word "training" in relation to cats isn't quite correct. Training implies submission, which implies force. Your cat will not tolerate this attitude; it will only do as it pleases. Imagine your cat as your little furry child for a moment. Would you hit your child? Similarly, you shouldn't hit your feline friend, or pressure it to perform for you.

2. Cats are creatures of often seemingly fickle temperament. If you push, they will push in response. If you shout or hit they will remember the offense for the rest of their lives and take revenge at the first opportunity. Don't be fooled because your feline's brain is only about the size of a walnut. They are incredibly smart and complex creatures full of passion. Be a friend and partner to your feline, and they will be the same to you.

3. You may use the same commands used by circus trainers in their circus acts, but it is not the commands themselves that are important here, but the timbre and intonation of the voice giving the commands. It is also worth using commands that naturally appear less in your everyday vocabulary. Overexposure to a command word outside of the training context can confuse your animal.

4. Speak to your cat as though it's your little child. Many already consider their cats to be true members of their families, often even giving them human names. You wouldn't speak rudely to your child, even if you are in a bad mood because your boss yelled at you at work. Speak to your cat like you would your child: calmly and gently. Slowly and clearly pronounce every word, carefully looking them in the eyes. Do you think your pet doesn't

understand you? They understand, perhaps not the exact words, but the intonation with which you speak.

5. It has been suggested that a dog has the intelligence of a two-year-old child. Could cats be any worse? They will happily play with you. After all, in nature, cats even play with their prey before eating them. Take advantage of their willingness to play! Give your cat a command and play with them as cats are natural-born mentalists. They can understand your mood and desires for them, and this is highly advantageous at the intersection of their training and playing.

6. When dealing with a cat do not forget that nature has bestowed it with wonderful abilities. Cats can acutely feel the emotional state of their owners. Just petting relieves stress and normalizes blood pressure. Cats can sense the approach of a tsunami or earthquake. No wonder they were idolized in Ancient Egypt. Our felines should not be treated as an object to be trained, but as a domestic deity. If a stray cat appears on your doorstep, it is a good sign. Do not turn it away.

WHAT INTERESTS YOUR CAT?

Cat lovers know that their fluffy creatures will not obey a human. They will only do exactly what interests them, what they themselves want, not what their owners want. Do you want to train your cat? Start by learning its character and temperament.

The commands "sit" and "lie down" can be learned by male and female cats of any breed. However, female cats are smarter and cleverer than their male counterparts and will successfully adapt to the litter box faster than males.

WHEN SHOULD YOU TRAIN YOUR CAT?

Of course, it is best to work with your kitten from four to eight months. At that age it is already smart enough to remember tricks. Additionally, its individual habits haven't yet been solidified and will not interfere with its learning. You can try to train your adult pet as well, but keep in mind that major results will require more time.

BASIC CONDITIONS FOR SUCCESSFUL TRAINING

1. Buy your kitten toys, otherwise it will play with and chew everything it can get its paws and teeth: your shoes, furniture, etc.

2. Give your pet a private place to sleep and relax: a special bed, Ottoman, maybe a box with soft bedding. Without a private spot, your cat will rest where it sees fit, be it your chairs, the sofa, beds, etc. As a last resort, if your animal has already made your chair its top choice and does not want to leave, throw down a blanket so the fur and claws don't ruin the upholstery.

3. Don't scold a kitten. It will not understand the reason for your admonishment anyway. Speak to your kitten in a firm voice, as you would a child. Felines are smart animals, and they will quickly remember that if their owner is dissatisfied the behavior eliciting the dissatisfaction will not do.

4. Your kitten should have personal dishes for food and water from birth. Do not feed your pet from the table, as doing so will confuse it and encourage negative food habits. Remember, human food is bad for a cat's stomach, and you don't want your pet climbing on the table in search of food in your absence.

5. The litter box should always be in the same accessible place. If it's in the bathroom, always leave the door open. Change the litter regularly. If the litter is dirty, your pet will simply find another place in your home to use the bathroom, and it may turn out to be a pretty good hiding spot.

6. Do you want your training to be successful and effective? Be your pet's friend first. Spend more time with them, talk to them, play with them, pet them, and give them scratches behind the ears. Animals, like people, love affection.

HOW TO START TRAINING

The best way to begin training is by learning more about your pet. First, observe the animal: what kind of food does it like best? Meat? Fish? Dry food? Learn the time you can spend on a training session with your cat. How long will it tolerate playing and practicing?

Figure out at what times of day your pet is the most active, and at what times they prefer to sleep. Domestic cats are also predators, albeit small, and in nature, wild cats predators spend most of their time half-asleep, watching for prey. So will their domestic counterparts, napping on the windowsill in the sun.

Your observations will help you achieve results without much effort.

Take a close look at your pet. What does it do on its own without your training or influence? Does it love to take a ball of paper in its teeth and carry it back and forth? If so, it can certainly learn to fetch.

And if your cat loves to jump, you can try to teach it to jump through a hoop or onto your shoulder. If your cat naturally extends a fluffy paw to you for attention or to ask for food, it can certainly learn to shake. Learning is best started with the most basic and natural commands and actions. Only after this should you move on to more complex exercises.

Keep in mind that when an animal does not like something, it is almost impossible to force it to act. It is important to handle training like a kind of game and method of communication between owner and pet. The earliest training should be started by getting your animal used to its name and the litter box.

DAILY EDUCATION OF YOUR FURRY COMPANION

It's not particularly important whether you purchased your kitten or whether it was born within your cat family; teach it to use the litter box as soon as possible. Each animal must have its own litter box.

Place your kitten in its box five to seven minutes after feeding. A single time should suffice for your kitten. It will remember the odor and remember where it should use the bathroom. This habit will become ingrained for the rest of your pet's, alas, short (by human standards) life. It may arise that your pet refuses to go in the designated place, opting instead for the floor, sink, bath, or one of your shoes. Do not punish your kitten for this. You need to figure out why. Perhaps the blame lies with the owner, and not the pet. It could be that your kitten doesn't like the litter; it may give off an unpleasant odor. It could also be that your cat doesn't like the location of the litter box (be sure to choose a secluded place). Additionally, it could be that the litter needs to be cleaned and replaced more frequently.

TRAINING YOUR CAT TO USE THE TOILET

The dream of any owner is that their cat goes to the bathroom in the toilet. There would be no need to have a litter box. The unwanted odors in the apartment would be far more pleasant. If the cat shows interest in the toilet itself, it might suggest that your pet would be able to learn to use the toilet. This is worth trying to teach.

1. Place the litter box next to the toilet.
2. Elevate the box a little more each day until it is as high as the toilet bowl.
3. When your cat has become accustomed to going at the height of the toilet bowl, replace the litter box with a special box that attaches inside the toilet. Be sure to buy flushable litter!
4. Gradually increase the size of the hole in the training box until the cat learns to do its business on the toilet. Remove the box.
5. Don't forget to praise your cat for every success!

Of course, your pet must have a name it recognizes as its own. With kittens, the matter is pretty simple. They will learn their names naturally and quickly. Of course, if your kitten is purebred, and its pedigree name takes up an entire line of paper, it should be reduced as much as possible to avoid confusing the little one. You don't need to specifically train your kitten to remember its name. Simply call your pet by name every time you pour food into its bowl, and it will learn its name very quickly.

But what if there is a new, adult animal in the house that doesn't yet have a name? How should you call your new pet? Most cats will respond to the tried and true "Here-kitty-kitty-kitty." When you settle on a name for your pet, just like with a kitten, put food in the bowl and call it. If it doesn't respond, try calling "Here-kitty-kitty." Now repeat the trick. Do it several times and your new pet will quickly figure out the connection between your calling it and its food.

SCIENTIFIC JUSTIFICATION OF TRAINING

Russian scientist I.P. Pavlov proved, through his experiments with dogs, that the core of any training of both animals and people are conditioned reflexes.

Reflexes can be divided into two groups:

1. Unconditioned reflexes, like the sucking reflex in newborn kittens. Though their eyes are still closed, they still seek out their mother to feed. Without this reflex, an animal would be doomed to die. It's also interesting to watch

how diligently little kittens wash their paws and clean behind their ears. They were not taught how to do this, for it is also an innate reflex.

2. Learned reflexes, which arise in response to some action, can be developed through training. For example, a pet will develop a conditioned reflex to the smell of cooking food or the rattling of a pot and associate those senses with their next meal. Oftentimes a cat will even develop a reflex to its owner simply entering the kitchen and will follow them in, expecting to be fed.

An interesting point: a learned reflex can form an unconditioned one. If you feed your pet at the same time every day, as, in principle, is correct and necessary to do, the production of stomach acid will begin not when the cat eats, but earlier, at the moment you start preparing the food, or rustling the bag of dry food.

HOW TO RAISE AN OBEDIENT CAT

In training, there are such basic concepts including:

1. A conditional command. When called, your pet performs a certain action. A conditional command can be a sound or some other sensed perception picked up by your feline, connected to the intonation of your voice or a specific place or time.

2. Reinforcement, in both positive and negative forms. Negative reinforcement is punishing your pet. To cause it pain or shouting at it should never be used. Positive reinforcement, on the other hand, is feeding your pet its

favorite food or showing your loved one affection through words and scratches behind the ears. Positive reinforcement always works better than negative reinforcement in training your pet. Remember: "A kind word and a cat is pleased."

A note for comparison: to completely train a person requires about 25 repetitions, and for animals, anywhere from 22 to 205. Dogs are typically far easier to train than cats, requiring an average of 15-50 training sessions, while cats average 55-100 sessions. These are approximate figures, of course, and depend on the individual characteristics of each person or animal.

HOW TO AVOID MISTAKES WHEN WORKING WITH YOUR PET

What is the goal of a pet owner? To form your pet's conditioned reflexes in response to stimuli, like your voice or food. Training sessions should be conducted when both you and your pet are in a good mood, and your pet should not be very hungry, though it will respond more to treats when it is. The most effective training will happen when both owner and pet want to relax and play.

Your training sessions do not require any special facilities or conditions. In fact, it's best to practice at home in an environment familiar to your animal. Training should be conducted as follows: your pet does something and receives a reward. Pet your cat. Give it scratches and an affectionate word or treat, or both.

If your pet does not want to obey your commands, do not use force. It will run from you, hide somewhere, and no longer respond to your requests. Do not repeat the same command 100 times. Your cat will get tired, and you will discourage it from learning. The optimal duration of a training session with your cat is around five minutes.

If you want to achieve the best results, do a day of several sessions that last around five minutes, then take a long break until the next day. Your cat will gradually form a response to your commands if proper training conditions are respected.

TRAINING METHODS

There are several training methods based on knowledge of the basics of the learned reflex:

1. Negative reinforcement, which causes pain to the animal, can involve food deprivation, shouting, and violence. They are inhumane ways to treat an animal and are completely ineffective. The only time an owner should act in the realm of negative reinforcement is when their pet is doing something potentially harmful to itself or its owner or other family members.

2. Positive reinforcement is the more effective method to train your pet. You need to encourage your animal, praise it loudly, pet it affectionately, rub its belly, and give it a treat.

3. "Do as I do." A mother cat always teaches her kittens the skills of adult life. If she doesn't catch mice, neither will her kittens. Therefore, a kitten and its mother should not be separated too early. There are interesting examples of kittens raised in a home with puppies. Growing up with dogs, these kittens developed a dog's mannerisms and behavior. Try to set an example for your kittens. Just don't bark or meow at them.

4. An integrated approach utilizes the other three approaches at the same time and can be the fastest, most effective way to see results when training certain animals. Remember, however, that negative reinforcement methods are *ineffective* in training your felines, and will most likely harm the relationship you have, or hope to have, with them.

WHAT IS NEEDED FOR TRAINING?

For successful training you will need:

1. Unlimited patience and time. Do not forget that a reflex is formed when your animal recognizes the actions you *want* it to perform, and not through rote repetition and simple memorization of an action. Do not torment your pet with overtraining. Keep your sessions to around five minutes a day.

2. Full trust between animal and owner. If a cat shows open disdain for its owner, there is no hope of its training. Sometimes it's just that a pet and an owner simply don't get along. An animal should not be punished for this.

3. Your cat's favorite food, in sufficient quantity and fresh, especially if it's meat, fish, or cheese. When training, try to always use the same treat. If possible, never change. When rewarding your pet don't give it too much as this will confound the pet and the training will be disrupted or stop working.

Food should be soft and small, so that your cat understands it's a reward for its work, and not food for sustenance.

As a treat, buy food that is not usually a part of your cat's diet. If you usually feed your cat wet food, get dry food as a treat, and vice versa. The reward should be given immediately upon completion of the task, and the cat should finish the entire treat. If you are late with a treat, or your cat is slow to finish it, the feline will lose the association you create with the job-well-done.

When your pet has learned the trick, try to wean it off the treat. First give a treat for each completed command, then every other, then every third, etc. Keep the distribution to a minimum when your cat has learned the trick, but feel free to pet your cat and praise them as much as you want.

TIPS FROM EXPERIENCED TRAINERS:

1. Conduct training sessions regularly. If this is not possible, then at least throughout a single day, or a couple days. Even once-weekly repetition can be sufficient for a cat to learn a trick.

2. Never deceive your cat. If a treat was promised, you must give it, even if the command has already been learned entirely.

3. Praise your cat with the same words. Try to use words not normal to everyday conversations so your pet doesn't get confused.

4. Never show violence to your pet. Only love, patience and affection will bring results.

5. Training is best done in the morning on an empty stomach.

6. Training methods should be consistent from the simplest to the most complex tasks.

TRAINING
IS PLAYING

If you really want to train your cat, you must invest play time. And they love to play, especially kittens. Just like a child, a cat will play with you when it is healthy, happy, and not hungry. Never try to force your cat to play with you.

Cats are best trained using the positive reinforcement method. For some, delicious treats are a good option. For the most active cats and kittens, a favorite toy can be suitable for strengthening a reflex. The oldest cats are often indifferent to treats and toys but are smart and love their owners as positive reinforcement shows them lots of physical affection.

Depending on the breed, some cats are not as prone to instances of hyperactivity throughout their lives. If your cat doesn't respond to treats, toys, or physical affection, review your list of commands. A stoic cat will not likely run, jump, or stand on its hind legs. Try some of the less involved commands with it like shaking a paw, sitting, and lying down. A hungry animal will be more willing to exercise than one that has just eaten and has a full belly.

Remember that cats are not dogs. You will have to spend more time training your cat. The reason is not that dogs are smarter than cats, but that cats can have unpredictable temperaments. If your cat doesn't want to do something, no amount of treats, praise, yelling, or affection will make it perform.

WHERE TO BEGIN

Start with the most basic command. They should be pronounced calmly and slowly, enunciating every word. Cats are very sensitive to intonation. There are a few tricks to help you develop each of these commands with your cat. Remember that the specific command words are not overly important, but, to avoid confusing your feline, they should be words not used overly much in daily life. Let's look at each trick in detail:

1.   "Come!"

Take a treat or your cat's favorite toy and call it by name. Food is more effective if your training session is before your pet's meal. When your cat comes running, give it the treat followed with petting. Gradually move away from your cat and repeat the trick in different rooms several times a day.

2. Stay!

Work on this command when your pet is already stationery. Bend down and say the command loudly. Praise the cat when it doesn't move, pet it, and give it a treat. Try moving around the room and repeating the command when stopping at a new location.

3. Jump!

a. With a ring or hoop:

To work with an adult cat, a small hoop will be useful, and for training a kitten, an embroidery hoop works perfectly. To train your cat, place the hoop between it and the reward. Coax it through the hoop with the treat. As soon as your cat steps through the hoop, give it the treat and use positive reinforcement. Repeat this until your cat will freely walk through the hope without reward. Now begin gradually lifting the hoop off the floor so your cat must jump through. At the same time, clearly give your command. Keep raising the hoop until your cat has learned the connection between the command and jumping through the hoop.

b. From table to tablePut your cat or kitten on a chair, table, or nightstand.

1. Place another piece of furniture near enough for your cat's jump. Place a treat on the second piece of furniture and make sure your cat can clearly see the treat.
2. Your cat will jump for the treat, at which time you should give your command. Give your pet positive reinforcement after it completes the trick.

4. Sit

It is worth teaching your cat to sit for visits to the veterinarian. Or in case you ever want to photograph them. There are two primary ways to train this command:

First variant:

a. Show your cat a treat and call it to you.
b. When it approaches, raise your hand slightly above its head and say "Sit!"

Second variant:

a. If your cat is spinning at your feet, tap it lightly on the butt and say "Sit!"

b. Snap your fingers loudly to get your cat's attention.

c. Try simultaneously giving the command while you snap with one hand and tap your cat on the butt with the other hand.

5. Fetch

All cats carry their kittens with their mouths. So, in principle, you should be able to teach your cat this trick if they will already carry something around themselves. Kuri bobtails, Norwegian forest cats, and Cornish Rexes are known for this behavior. It is not accidental and is somewhat like the behavior of dogs.

a) Play with the cat with a small toy, a candy wrapper, piece of paper, or ball.
b) Throw it to one side.
c) Your pet will run after it and try to bring it back. At the moment it takes the toy in its teeth, say your command.
d) Praise your pet and give it a treat.
e) Repeat the exercise several times.
f) Over time, the cat will learn to fetch when it wants a treat.

6. Lie down!

If you want a hassle-free visit to the veterinarian with your cat, practice this command.

a) Put your cat next to you.
b) Show it a treat.
c) Slowly lower the treat.
d) As your cat's head lowers with the treat, move it slightly to one side and give your command.
e) As soon as the cat lies down, give it the treat and praise.

7. Shake

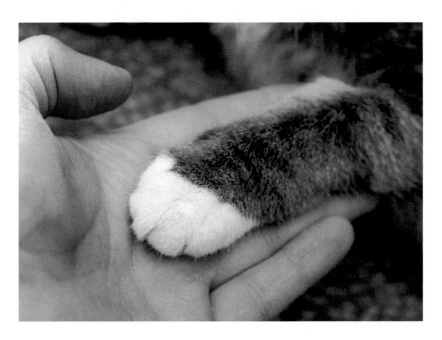

a) Place a treat in your palm or close it in your fist. Let your cat smell the treat.
b) Your cat will try to reach out with its paw.

c) Hold your cat's paw on your hand and say your command.
d) Give the treat and praise.
e) Repeat the exercise 3-5 times.

8. Sit pretty

a) Let your cat smell the treat in your hand.
b) Slowly raise your hand.
c) Your cat should intuitively reach for the treat and stand on its hind legs.
d) Say your command and give your cat the treat.

9. Crawl

a) Choose a time when your cat is already lying down.
b) Pet it with one hand, <u>gently</u> holding it against the floor, not allowing it to get up.
c) Move the treat away from your cat's nose, and they will be forced to crawl towards the treat.
d) Reward your pet with the treat.

10. Roll over

a) Get your cat's attention when it is already lying down.
b) Hold the treat above your cat, near the area of the shoulder blades.
c) Attracted by the smell, your cat will start to turn its head back towards the treat.
d) With one hand, tap your cat on the side or neck, encouraging it to roll over. Move the treat back and your cat should complete the trick.
e) Praise your cat and give it the well-deserved treat.

11. Speak

a) To practice this command, wait until your cat is hungry.
b) Tease your cat a little, allowing it to smell the food.
c) When it begins to meow and demand the food, give your command, followed by the food and praise.

HOW TO HARNESS TRAIN YOUR CAT

For some, the very image of a cat walking on a leash may seem funny, but in a fast-moving world with many less-than-careful drivers on the roads, letting your pet roam freely outside can be a dangerous move. Buy your feline a special walking harness made for them. Do not use a simple dog leash and collar, or you risk causing bodily harm to your furry friend.

1. Put the harness on your pet. Let it get used to it by walking around the house.
2. Fasten the leash to the harness and continue to walk your cat, remaining in your home.
3. Progress from your home to your yard as your cat adjusts to the new harness.
4. Always encourage your cat with kind touches and words.
5. Increase the distance and scope of your walks as works for your cat.
6. Remember, many cats will be frightened of dogs and attempt to bolt when seeing them.
7. Never walk near highways, freeways, or particularly noisy roads.

TRAINING FOR DIFFERENT BREEDS

There are certain breeds of cats that are naturally less active than others: the calm and thoughtful stoics, which have a mind entirely of their own. As such, they are harder to train than their more curious, hyperactive counterparts. British shorthairs, for example, are usually more reserved and easygoing; your sedate British is unlikely to madly chase after a ball.

On the contrary, the ever-mobile, restless Bengals, Abyssinians, bobtails, and sphinxes will happily play with their owners. Successfully training a Maine

Coon, Angora, Russian blue, or Persian will require an owner to use all their knowledge, experience, and training tricks. They are some of the calmest, but also the most independent breeds.

Russian cat trainer Yuri Kuklachev believes they can be trained all the same, but not like other animals. Cats will understand some commands before you've said half a word but may not react to other commands at all. Every furry creature requires an individual approach to its education, just like people. In training your cat, try to teach it only the tricks it truly enjoys performing. Every cat, however, should be able to learn its own name and how to use its litter box. The methods of coercion and punishment are not acceptable or conducive to training your cat effectively.

FIVE EXCELLENT STUDENTS: THE EASIEST BREEDS TO TRAIN

ABYSSINIAN

One of the most loyal and faithful breeds, Abyssinians are very curious, sociable, and fearless. They do not fear water, will very rarely keep you up with their yowling, and are quick, goofy, and always ready to play. Their muscular body and long paws make it easier for them to perform certain tricks like jumps and somersaults. They also respond very well to retrieval commands; they love to return a thrown toy to play more with their owners. Abyssinians will not allow you to become bored. Come up with any game you'd like, and your Abyssinian will be happy to play with you.

AMERICAN SHORTHAIR

American shorthairs are known for their calm, reserved characters. They like to play, but no roughhousing. They do not like to be squeezed or jostled. American shorthairs are typically silent, meowing very rarely, and make excellent hunters. They are most effectively trained in a playful manner, but only when there's complete trust between them and their owners.

BENGAL

Bengals are one of the newest cat breeds. They are at the same time independent and sociable, and often affectionate. They purr very loudly and meow endlessly. If you have pet birds, mice, or hamsters, you should not have a Bengal in the house, as it will try to hunt your other pets. Bengals are agile, hyperactive, and muscular cats that do not fear water. They are incredibly smart, adjust well to training, and live longer than many other breeds.

SIAMESE

Siamese cats are distinguished by their loyalty to their owners, like dogs. If you have a Siamese at home, don't be surprised when it tags along with you wherever you go. Siamese like to have fun zooming around the house, running through everything in their paths, until they suddenly freeze. If the house is quiet and your Siamese is calm it may sit nicely and watch TV. Siamese learn with pleasure and will perform commands tirelessly.

SAVANNAH

The Savannah, first bred by crossing a wild African Serval with a domestic cat, is the most expensive cat breed. They have short to medium length hair and often have tabby or black coats. Savannah cats are some of the smartest. They have retained some of their wild tendencies and love to be out in the open air or water. They can coexist calmly with other animals, adore their owners, and love to play. Savannah cats are a pleasure to train and can learn the most complex commands.

These five breeds are some of the best representatives of cats that can be most easily trained, but there are many more. Even the most unremarkable kittens from a domestic cat can perform many tricks with pleasure. Therefore, it is not necessary to spend a lot of money on a breed considered more trainable. It is far more effective to pay attention to the furry little friends living under your roof. Train effectively and proactively and you will achieve results with your cat and/or her kittens, regardless of breed.

It is believed that, in addition to the five previously mentioned breeds, there is another type of cat with special characteristics conducive to effective training. This type of feline, however, does not belong to any one breed, and may be born of any mother cat. These are the so-called Hemingway cats, or polydactyls, felines born with extra toes on their paws, sometimes up to eight on a single paw. But it's not just the number of toes that make them different.

Hemingways often display different behavior and habits than their normal 18-toed counterparts. They are considered to be more intelligent and highly trainable. How is it that Hemingways came to be? And how is it that you can find Hemingways born into any litter, regardless of how many toes their mother may have? A genius kitten can be born into any breed; you may already have one at home. But how can you identify your star pupil to select for training?

WHERE DID HEMINGWAY'S FURRY GENIUSES COME FROM?

As previously mentioned, Hemingway cats are not a breed; they may be born into any breed. But why are any cats born with extra toes in the first place? Is this simply a genetic mutation or one of Mother Nature's great mysteries? Where was the first six-toed kitten born? Why are they considered mysterious and highly intelligent?

Biologists studying domestic cats are still unsure of the exact origin of polydactyl cats. Polydactyls are rarer to come by in Europe as most of them were killed in the Middle Ages, having been considered messengers of the devil. Across the Atlantic in North America, however, these unusual creatures lived quietly and multiplied.

Polydactyls have taken an interest in Key West Island in particular. It's always warm, but the heat is never blistering. This natural anomaly can be explained by the fact that ocean waters around the island maintain almost the same temperature year-round. Inhabitants of the island are sure that these beautiful cats, which settled on the island thanks to Ernest Hemingway, bring happiness and good fortune to Key West.

ERNEST HEMINGWAY: "I WANT A SIX-TOED CAT!"

If you think back a little, the reason for Hemingway's desire becomes clear. The writer once heard a legend about cats with six toes on their front paws from a sailor. According to the sailor, these polydactyls not only protected the ship and crew from disasters on their trips around the world, but also brought luck and love to the sailors.

Captain Stanley Dexter, owner of a six-toed cat and lover of literature, often met with Hemingway during his layovers on Key West. He learned that Hemingway was very interested in these special cats.

During his next visit to Key West, the captain brought his unusual kitten as a gift for Hemingway.

The cat was a Maine Coon named Snow White for its pure, white fur. "Let her catch luck and bring it into your home," the captain said to his friend as he handed over the cat.

This is how the first six-toed cat appeared in Hemingway's famous home on Key West island in Florida. After some time, there were between 150-200 cats freely roaming around the writer's estate. After Hemingway's death, a museum was created in the home. Today, about 70 cats still live on the estate.

An interesting fact: every third tourist coming to Key West makes their first stop at Hemingway's house of cats, wishing to see the special, extra-toed grandchildren and great-grandchildren of Snow White, Hemingway's first polydactyl. Hemingway continued the tradition established with Snow White and gave his cats names of celebrities or characters from books.

These special felines with their abnormally large paws have many fans all over the world. Like Hemingway, many believe that these cats bring good luck and prosperity to their home.

The polydactyls on Key West are not afraid of people. They move freely around the estate as though they own the place. The curator of the Hemingway museum remarked at how quietly the six-toed felines tolerate stressful situations. They do not run and hide and will let you pet them and take a picture as a souvenir.

All the furry inhabitants of the Hemingway estate have six toes on their front paws, and some have even been born with extra toes on their back paws, though this is rare for polydactyls. These cats are otherwise ordinary in appearance and are if various colors and sizes. Hemingway's cats live long lives on Key West, sometimes reaching twenty years old. In the far corner of the estate lies a special cemetery for the cats.

Every cat gets its own name, and all of them seem to respond to their names. The Key West Hemingways are very attached to those who care for them and give the museum a special atmosphere, as the estate must have had during the writer's life.

Cats were always one of Hemingway's passions. He believed cats sincerely show their feelings, openly express themselves, and always maintain their independence, no matter how much they love their owners.

Sailors shared the writer's love of polydactyl cats and were certain that keeping the special felines would bring luck. Also, extra claws helped to catch the mice on the ships. The wider paws of polydactyls also made it easier for them to balance on the rocking deck of a ship and earned them the nickname "mitten paws."

THE AMAZING WORLD OF POLYDACTYLS

What exactly does polydactyl mean? From the Latin meaning "many digits," there are several varieties: Some may have extra toes only on their back paws; some are the opposite. Other polydactyls may have seven toes on their front paws and six toes on their back paws, and vice versa, of course. Very rarely are polydactyls born with eight toes on any of their paws, but it is possible.

At first glance, it may appear that these cats are wearing mittens or snowshoes on their paws. Many polydactyls carry their extra toes on the inside of their paws, giving them the appearance of having thumbs. The length of their digits can vary, and two toes of varying length might be right next to each other on one paw. It is impossible to look at these fluffy felines in their mittens without smiling.

The Guinness world record for the most digits on a feline belongs to a Canadian cat named Jake, who has 28 toes on his four paws. Most often, a polydactyl feline will have 24 toes between its four paws, but any number of extra toes means a unique and special cat is in your presence.

What causes polydactyly in cats? Polydactyly is an inherited trait, meaning a mother cat with extra toes is more likely to give birth to offspring that also have an abnormal number.

How rare are polydactyls? Polydactyls can be found in large numbers on Key West, of course, the east coast of the United States, Wales, and the southwest United Kingdom.

It is believed they first arrived in North America on ships from England and Wales. This explains why polydactyly appears in Maine Coons, which inhabit the east coast in great numbers.

CHARACTERISTICS OF POLYDACTYLS

The multi-toed Maine coon is often friendly and very sociable, while a polydactyl Siamese cat is often very vocal and curious.

Polydactyls will largely behave like ordinary cats. They can be playful, shy, mischievous, friendly, and curious. Having extra toes does not mean your cat will have any other special character traits, but their polydactyly will still give them an advantage over their normal packmates. A polydactyl's "mitten-clad" paws help it open doors and drawers more easily. Those felines blessed with pronounced "thumbs" can grip things more effectively. These extra abilities of a polydactyl ensure that one's life as an owner will never be boring.

BLESS YOU, MITTENS!

Polydactyly is a congenital anomaly, and the fact that your cat is born with extra toes does not mean it will be beset with serious health issues. In level of activity and willingness to play, your polydactyl shouldn't differ much from other cats of its breed.

Polydactyls are not so different from normal cats. The only extra danger they might face is a person accidentally stepping on their bigger paws or catching their paws on something sharp, requiring a visit to the veterinarian. Additionally, it is possible for a cat's extra digits to grow at off angles, causing problems with their claws and skin. In most cases, polydactyls are healthy, however, and have an average life expectancy. On the other hand, the extra toes are often beneficial to the cat, giving the paws a larger surface area, improving its ability to grip things. Because of this, polydactyls are often more successful hunters.

DON'T BREAK TRADITION!

Ernest Hemingway observed a tradition of naming his cats after literary heroes and celebrities. How did he pick the name? By letting his kittens grow up a little and observing their unique character traits, Hemingway would then choose a suitable name based on similarities to some character or famous person. Two particularly beautiful Hemingways were named after Marilyn Monroe and Audrey Hepburn. One feline with a particularly plush tail was named after President Harry Truman. Like his namesake, Hemingway found the cat to be very insistent and determined to get attention.

Hemingway considered another cat to be a true aristocrat among his pack, the spitting image of Winston Churchill. Like the former UK prime minister, Churchill the cat enjoyed fine food. This naming tradition maintained by Hemingway is preserved in the museum to this day.

Polydactyls can be referred to by many names including boxers, mitten paws, and Hemingways. The latter nickname is most often reserved for a single breed: the large Maine Coon. Hemingway's felines have always lived freely on the estate and continue to roam the grounds to this day.

WHAT SHOULD I NAME MY FURRY FRIEND?

What you name your feline depends entirely on your own imagination. You can take the easy route and go with Boots, Mittens, Felix, or Mr. Whiskers. Or you can try taking a page from Hemingway's book and coming up with a suitable name for your pet based on their personality. If you're blessed with a polydactyl, maybe try a derivative of the word itself, or another name that pays tribute to your cat's special paws.

Or you could honor Hemingway by naming your cat after him or adopting his naming tradition and choosing a character from one of his works, thereby demonstrating your knowledge of the history of these special extra-toed cats.

Or you could even honor Captain Stanley Dexter, who gave Hemingway his first polydactyl, by naming your kitten after him or choosing a name related to the sea.

A POLYDACTYL IN EVERY HOME!

Yes, in every home, among its furry inhabitants, you may find one of these special relatives of Hemingway's cats. Many like their big paws, sometimes giving the cat the appearance of a small bear. Veterinarians say that polydactyls often calmly sit in their arms, welcome petting and scratches, and are very sociable.

It is hard to disagree with Ernest Hemingway that these cats with their big paws are some of the most charming, fluffy creatures around. If you want to train your polydactyl, you will almost certainly find success.

CONCLUSION - HOW YOU SHOULD PLAY AND TRAIN

Members of the feline tribe do not like to be forced into action against their wishes. They do not tolerate orders or impositions of their owners' thoughts and desires. But, at the same time, our cats love us and are devoted to us. Otherwise, why would they come back, in some cases traveling hundreds of miles to return to their families.

Though they might not always show it openly, we know our felines love us. The desire to train your new cat is something positive, but, as you may have learned from this book, try starting by simply being friends with your pet. Friendship with your cat begins with a smile, a gentle touch, and treats. Establish a warm relationship with your pet and watch how faithfully it will greet you at home, like a child greets a parent returning home from work, rushing up to you, sticking its nose in your bag wondering what you might have brought.

Treat your kitten like a child. Through playing with your kitten, you will learn more about the specific games it likes and dislikes. Gradually, you can move from games to commands, but never lose your playful spirit, and do not forget that you should teach your kitten the skills they first show an interest in, not the skills you want them to learn most.

I believe you will succeed. Together with your pet partner, you can achieve the results you dream of. The ideal circumstances are when your wishes coincide with the wishes of your feline. Your joint effort in playing and training will make your life more beautiful, interesting, and fun. The most important thing is that both the owner and pet feel fulfilled when they spend time with one another.

Yes, cats are independent and self-sufficient animals. It is usually enough to put out some food and water and show them where they should use the bathroom. However, your cat will miss you when you're busy doing your own thing. They'll listen to you without interruption and will never divulge your secrets. They'll lie down next to the computer while you work, waiting impatiently for you to finish and come play.

Life would be much more boring without all our furry little friends of all colors, sizes, and numbers of toes walking the Earth by our sides. Cats are a blessing to people, so play with your cat, train your cat, but never forget:

"You become responsible for what you've tamed."

Antione de Saint-Exupery,

"The Little Prince"

I LOVE CATS

Leave Review

As an independent author with a small marketing budget, reviews are my livelihood on this platform.

If you enjoyed this book, i'd appreciate it if you could leave your honest feedback.You can do it by clicking the link below.

I read Every single review because I love the feedback from My readers!

Thank you for buying this book!

Made in the USA
Monee, IL
06 December 2020

51198904R00062